The Dust Bowl
Through the Lens

HOW PHOTOGRAPHY REVEALED AND
HELPED REMEDY A NATIONAL DISASTER

Martin W. Sandler

WALKER & COMPANY

New York

Introduction

The book you are about to read explores a unique time in American history. It is a story of hardship and disaster. But it is also the story of the extraordinary courage and spirit of millions of men, women, and children battling to survive against the forces of nature and man-made catastrophe.

There had never been anything like it. Between 1930 and 1936, more than 100 million acres of the most fertile land in America—land that the farm families of the southern plains had turned into the breadbasket of the world—turned to dust. Hundreds of thousands took to the road, desperately seeking to find new opportunities and build new lives thousands of miles away. Millions of others chose to remain and battle nature itself to save their land.

They were not alone. When the once-rich prairie was turned into a dust bowl, photography was still less than one hundred years old. Photographers were still discovering new possibilities for the camera. It would be in their portrayal of the Dust Bowl victims and their experiences that a special group of men and women would add a whole new dimension to what the camera could achieve.

As socially conscious as they were talented, these photographers were committed to accomplishing much more than simply recording people caught in a desperate situation. They saw the opportunity not only to inform the rest of the nation about what was happening but to bring about change through their photographs.

And they succeeded. Their pictures first shocked the government and then inspired it to take needed action, not only to bring relief to the Dust Bowl victims, but for the first time to take measures to restore and protect one of the nation's most precious resources—its soil.

We owe much to those who lived through the Dust Bowl. Their story reminds us once again of how Americans have responded with courage and determination in times of great crisis. And we owe much to the photographers whose pictures provide us with a permanent record of a remarkable time that must not be forgotten.

A Photographic Symbol

"There she sat in that lean-to tent with her children huddled around her, and seemed to know that my pictures might help her, and so she helped me." —DOROTHEA LANGE

The photograph on the opposite page is widely regarded as the very symbol of the Dust Bowl experience. Titled "Migrant Mother" by the photographer, Dorothea Lange, it is a prime example of the way in which photography both revealed almost every aspect of one of the most difficult times in American history and played a major role in bringing relief to the millions who had found themselves in a desperate situation.

Along with being one of the most compelling images ever taken, "Migrant Mother" also became one of the most influential. Printed in newspapers, magazines, and other publications around the nation, the photograph touched the hearts of millions far removed from the Dust Bowl.

Ironically, Lange almost missed taking the picture. She was on her way home for the night after photographing Dust Bowl migrants all day when she passed a sign that said Pea-Pickers Camp. For the next twenty miles she could not get the thought out of her head that she might have missed the chance to take an important picture. Finally, she turned around and drove all the way back to the camp, where, as she later wrote, "I saw and approached the hungry and desperate mother, as if drawn by a magnet."

That the picture became so famous was due not only to its compelling content but to Lange's artistry with a camera. Her framing of the image with the heads of the two children gave the picture the masterful composition that distinguishes every great photograph. By taking the picture at the moment the woman placed her hand on her chin in an obvious gesture of concern, she heightened the drama and impact of the photograph.

Above: *Determined to produce the most powerful image possible, Dorothea Lange took several photographs of the "Migrant Mother" other than the one that became so famous.*

Opposite: *Today, some seventy-five years after it was taken, "Migrant Mother" remains arguably the most recognizable photograph of all time.*

A Land of Plenty

We cross the prairie as of old
The pilgrims crossed the sea,
To make the West, as they the East,
The homestead of the free!

—JOHN GREENLEAF WHITTIER,
"THE KANSAS EMIGRANTS"

America has always been a land of opportunity. And that opportunity was never greater than in 1862 when the United States government passed the Homestead Act. At the time, most of the land in the United States west of the Mississippi River remained unsettled. The Homestead Act offered 160 acres of free land to anyone who would turn his new property into a working farm.

Into these prairie lands poured hundreds of thousands of Americans from the East—factory workers dissatisfied with the drudgery of their work and the low wages they earned, farmers frustrated with trying to eke out a living from the rocky eastern soil, and thousands of others eager to fulfill the dream of owning their own land. They were joined by hordes of oppressed emigrants from Europe, anxious to take advantage of the offer of free land in a free country.

By 1900, more than eighty million acres of land on the American plains had been settled and more than 370,000 farms had been created. These brave pioneers had endured incredible hardships—scorching heat in summer, raging blizzards in winter, devastating invasions of insects, and constant winds. But the Great Plains contained some of the richest soil in the world, and the dawn-to-dusk efforts of the entire family, who even had to build their first homes out of blocks made from the tough prairie soil, enabled them to plant and harvest the abundant crops that would feed not only America but the rest of the world.

By 1930, all of these western farm people could look with satisfaction on what had been accomplished. "To me it was breath-taking," Kansas farmer Lawrence Svobida wrote, "the most beautiful scene in all the world; and hundreds of acres of that wheat was mine."

Above: *Keeping up with the abundance of wheat and other grains that the rich soil yielded required the labor of every member in a prairie farm family.*

Opposite: *Realizing that this was their one chance to be recorded for posterity, most pioneer families made sure that prized possessions such as birdcages were included in the picture as they posed for the camera.*

Wheat Heaven

"Early and late, from all directions, has resounded the hum of tractors and combines. Trucks have been . . . carrying piled-up loads of bright, hard, full-kerneled wheat. . . . I have never seen a more beautiful harvest." —OKLAHOMA FARM WOMAN CAROLINE HENDERSON

"I believe," Kansas farmer Lawrence Svobida wrote, "any man must see beauty in mile upon mile of level land where the wheat, waist high, sways to the slightest breeze and is turning a golden yellow under a flaming July sun." His joy was understandable. For in the southern plains states in particular— Oklahoma, Kansas, Texas, Colorado, and New Mexico—wheat was the most valuable crop of all, the crop that most farmers in the region wanted to plant.

Plant it they did—with a vengeance. The great demand for wheat had begun in 1917 with the entry of the United States into World War I. Anxious to acquire as much wheat as possible to feed the troops and America's allies, the government guaranteed the southern plains farmers a payment of at least two dollars a bushel, a princely sum for those days. By the time the war ended in 1919, the rallying cries of "plant more wheat" and "wheat will win the war" had become well-known slogans and farmers were receiving more than four dollars a bushel for the crop.

By 1928, wheat had become the cornerstone of the economy of the southern plains, the pride of the entire region. "The Panhandle of Oklahoma," state senator W. J. Rizen would boast, "is destined to be the greatest wheat-growing country in the world."

He was right. Convinced that the good times would never end, southern plains farmers, not only in Oklahoma but throughout the region, turned an astounding amount of acreage into wheat. In the Texas Panhandle alone, two million acres of land were plowed up to grow the crop. So much land was plowed and so much wheat was grown that by 1930 the southern plains farmers had produced the largest wheat crop in history. No wonder that John McCarty, editor of the *Dalhart Texan*, would proudly proclaim, "This is the best [darn] country God's sun ever shone upon."

Above: *As this World War I poster indicates, wheat grown by the southern plains farmers was essential to the war effort.*

Opposite: *As the demand for wheat continued to increase, scenes like this one of farmers threshing huge quantities of the precious crop became commonplace throughout Oklahoma, Texas, Kansas, and neighboring states.*

Destroying the Land

"We just kept plowing. Our neighbors just kept plowing. We were all sure that the good times would never end." —TEXAS FARMER ABRAHAM KRAMES

Certain that wheat prices would continue to rise and confident that the beneficial rains so vital to the crops would continue to bless the region, southern plains farmers plowed up miles of the virgin prairie soil.

They had a great advantage over the homesteaders who had originally settled the land. Now they had the most advanced farm machinery yet developed—gasoline-powered tractors, heavy combines and threshers, trucks as well as horses and wagons—that made plowing and harvesting faster and more efficient than ever before.

Beginning in the early 1920s, they also had a new type of mechanical plow, a machine that would have a profound effect on the future of the region. It was called a "disc plow" and was very different from the plows that had originally broken the plains. The horse-driven plows of the earlier prairie settlers had cut deep down into the earth and sliced through the grass roots, barely breaking the precious topsoil and producing large clumps of earth that provided a barrier against the constant prairie winds. The disc plow, with its series of sharp vertical blades, cut much shallower into the earth and pulverized the topsoil into fine dirt.

The result was that after weeks of being disc plowed, a layer of dust settled on the fields. Anxious to plow as much acreage as quickly as possible, the farmers were unconcerned about this dust. They knew that the constant rains would keep it from being a problem. But the problem only grew worse. Looking out at the fields of accumulating dust and remembering how the farmers had made so much money without being concerned about what they were doing to the land, Kansas newspaperman William Allen White wrote, "His good times had ruined him."

Above: *By the beginning of the 1930s, although horses and other equipment-hauling animals were still being used, tractors were increasingly present in the fields.*

Opposite: *The heavy equipment made the lives of southern plains farmers much easier and more productive. The damage they did to the soil was a very different story.*

Prelude to Disaster

"By mid-August . . . we were feeding hay to the cattle because there was no grass left even along the roadside ditches." —NORTH DAKOTA FARM GIRL ANN MARIE LOW

Day after day, week after week, the farmers kept plowing, preparing the land for the planting of the profitable wheat. Even the poorest soil on their property was plowed in order to get as much wheat as possible. "My tractor roared day and night," Lawrence Svobida wrote, "and I was [plowing] eighty acres every twenty-four hours, only stopping for servicing once every six hours. I had a man driving from six in the morning until six in the evening. Then I would drive the [tractor] throughout the entire night."

Those who owned their farms were not the only ones who plowed up every available acre. With wheat prices so high, individuals from as far away as the East Coast began buying up whatever land in the region was available. Called "suitcase farmers" because they only occasionally visited the men whom they had hired to plant and harvest their wheat crop, they had even less concern for how the land was being torn up.

And the land was being destroyed in another way as well. Not all those who settled the southern plains concentrated on farming the land. The vast amount of acreage and the rich prairie grasses made the region ideal for raising sheep and cattle. By allowing their livestock to continually eat the grasses right down to the roots, the ranchers also contributed to destroying the soil. But they, like the farmers, were unconcerned. As it did for the overplowed land, the rains would restore the overgrazed land as well.

The farmers had turned their region into the greatest wheat-producing area in the world. The ranchers had raised millions of sheep and cattle. But they had unwittingly set the stage for an environmental disaster.

Above: *By the 1930s, the glory days of the American cowboy were long over. But there were still a significant number of cattle ranchers on the southern plains whose animals devoured enormous amounts of prairie grass.*

Opposite: *The presence of hundreds of sheep grazing peacefully on the open plains created a lovely, pastoral sight. But, like the cattle, the sheep were also playing a part in the destruction of the land.*

A Decade Without Rain

"We dream of the faint gurgling sound of dry soil sucking in the grateful moisture, but we wake to another day of wind and dust and hopes deferred," Oklahoma farm woman Caroline Henderson wrote. She was expressing a sentiment that was soon shared by all who lived in the Dust Bowl.

From 1931 to 1937 it stopped raining, creating a drought throughout the Great Plains that has never been equaled. With much of the topsoil having been pulverized by overplowing and much of the native grass that held the dirt in place having been destroyed by overgrazing, the soil was already in bad shape—even before a record drought set in. To make matters worse, the winters throughout that period were terribly dry as well, depriving the land of the benefits of the melting snow that would ordinarily be expected each spring.

The record drought was accompanied by record heat, further drying out the land. During one stretch in 1934, temperatures exceeded 100 degrees Fahrenheit for forty consecutive days, reaching as high as 118 degrees. Hundreds of people and livestock died from the heat.

As if all that was not enough, the winds throughout the long period were unusually strong. The tragic combination of drought, heat, and wind was turning the earth to dust. As historian Donald Worster wrote, "In no other instance was there [to be] greater or more sustained damage to the American land." He was right. The prairie soil, the lifeblood of the southern plains farmers, was about to blow away.

Above: *Perhaps nothing better revealed the devastation caused by the drought that plagued the southern plains than this photograph of the cracked, parched earth and sun-baked animal skull taken by photographer Arthur Rothstein.*

Opposite: *A boy looks out sadly at his family's all-important farmland, which has been devastated by wind and drought.*

Black Blizzard

"[We] were driving home . . . on this beautiful Sunday afternoon. [We] were caught out in the approaching storm. . . . We could see the cloud roll upon us as one might helplessly watch an approaching mountain avalanche." —TEXAS FARM GIRL KATHLEEN (ALLEN) LEWIS

*I*n September 1931, the most unusual natural occurrence in the lives of even the oldest residents of the southern plains took place. If there was one thing these people could expect, it was storms. Hailstorms, sandstorms, blizzards, tornadoes—they were all part of the challenges of living on the open prairie. But this storm was very different. The enormously high cloud it carried with it was pitch black, and rather than being blown along by the more than sixty-mile-per-hour winds, it seemed to roll over the land as if it had a mind of its own. "I remember that first bad dust storm," Nebraska resident Clara Lutkemeier would later recall. "The birds fluttered, the rabbits ran, and the sky turned black. We thought it was a [tornado], and we took to the cave and stayed for about an hour. When we got back to the house, the dust lay so thick in the back bedroom we just moved the mattress into the middle room so we could sleep."

As the storm made its way across Texas, Oklahoma, Kansas, Colorado, and New Mexico, perplexed citizens called the weather bureau, anxious to discover what was happening. The weather experts had no idea. They too had never seen anything like it. There was one thing, however, about which they seemed certain. This was a one-time phenomenon, a unique kind of storm that would not take place again.

Above: *A black blizzard approaches the center of Elkhart, Kansas.*

Opposite: *Liberal, Kansas, about to be engulfed by a dust storm. Within minutes, day was turned into night by the terrible storm.*

Endless Darkness

"This is ultimate darkness. So must come the end of the world." —KANSAS FARM WOMAN

In 1932, there were fourteen more of these black blizzards, and the weather bureau had officially given them the name "dust storms." By this time the millions of people who lived in the region had begun to realize that these storms threatened their very way of life. "The winds unleashed their fury with a force beyond anything we had previously experienced," Lawrence Svobida wrote after one of the "dusters."

In 1933, there were thirty-eight dust storms, and by 1934, when the storms started coming more frequently than ever, the residents of the southern plains states had become so familiar with them that they could actually tell in which state a particular duster had originated. If the dust it carried was black, it had begun with the lifting of the black soil of Kansas. If it was red, it had begun with the carrying away of the red soil of Oklahoma. If it was gray, it had originated in Colorado or New Mexico.

The people outside the southern plains were almost totally unaware of what was happening. But that all changed in the second week of May 1934, when a dust storm 1,500 miles long, 900 miles across, and two miles high dropped dirt as far away as New York City. A film of the dust was even deposited on President Herbert Hoover's desk in the White House. More astounding yet, prairie dust settled on ships 500 miles out in the Atlantic Ocean. "When people along the eastern seaboard began to taste fresh soil from the plains two thousand miles away," said government official Hugh Hammond Bennett, "many of them realized for the first time that somewhere, something had gone wrong with the land."

Above: *No town in the vast southern plains was spared from the continual dust storms. Here, a woman struggles to make her way to shelter as yet another duster strikes Amarillo, Texas.*

Opposite: *For motorists, being caught in a dust storm was truly terrifying. Here, a driver on a Texas highway attempts to make it home before being enveloped in a dust-caused blackout. Notice the dust piling up on the sides of the road like snow.*

An Alarming Situation

"We live with the dust, eat it, sleep with it, watch it strip us of possessions and the hope of possessions. . . . The nightmare is becoming life." —Dust Bowl resident Avis D. Carlson

Something had indeed gone wrong. Aside from the devastating loss of their crops, the people of the southern plains were consumed with battling the effects of the continual dusters. In almost every home, wet sheets were hung in front of the windows in an attempt to keep out the dust. Motorists were forced to drive with their headlights on even during the day. Railroad employees often had to walk in front of trains, scooping dust off the tracks so the train would not derail. During the first two years of the storms, teachers attempted to keep school in session by lighting lanterns so pupils could read their books. But after many instances of students and teachers being forced to stay in the schoolhouse overnight because of a sudden raging duster, many schools simply shut down.

"In the dust-covered desolation of our No Man's Land here . . . we have been trying to rescue our home from the wind-blown dust. . . . It is almost a hopeless task," one Oklahoma woman wrote. In some places the dust was so bad that housewives set out each meal not on top of a tablecloth but beneath it. When it was time to eat, each member of the family would duck his or her head under the cloth and eat their meal that way.

There were far more serious consequences as well. As the dust continued to pile up, an increasing number of people fell seriously ill or died from what became known as "dust pneumonia." As more and more people fell prey to the illness caused by continually breathing in the dust, hospitals became filled with dust pneumonia victims. In 1935, one-third of the deaths in just one county of Kansas alone were caused by dust pneumonia. At times throughout the region, more than fifty percent of all those admitted to hospitals were suffering from dust pneumonia. But what no one imagined was that the worst was yet to come.

Above: *With much of storeowners' merchandise ruined by the dust and with farmers struggling to eke out a living on their dust-covered fields, many towns like Caddo, Oklahoma, became almost totally abandoned.*

Opposite: *Fearful of contracting the dreaded dust pneumonia, many people took to wearing masks. Many also donned goggles to protect their eyes from the abrasive dust.*

Black Sunday

"Swirling in suddenly from the Southwest, the storm struck during a funeral at a local church, putting the crowd into a panic. Three people fainted as the dust swept inside the church."
—LIBERAL NEWS (LIBERAL, KANSAS)

At the end of March 1935, the southern plains were struck by a duster so large and destructive that by the time its fury was spent, it had destroyed one-quarter of the wheat crop in Oklahoma, half of the crop in Kansas, and all of it in Nebraska. It was only the beginning.

Sunday, April 14, 1935, dawned bright and beautiful all across the plains. Still reeling from the destruction caused by the March storm, people rushed outside to take advantage of the day. Suddenly, the temperature dropped as much as fifty degrees. Just as amazingly, people began to notice that hundreds of birds, frantically beating their wings and chattering nervously, were gathering in the yards around their homes as if they knew something ominous was about to happen.

They were right. As historian Donald Worster wrote, "Suddenly there appeared on the northern horizon a black blizzard, moving toward them; there was no sound, no wind, nothing but an immense 'boogery' cloud." It was the beginning of the most enormous dust storm of all, a duster that would carry with it more than 300,000 tons of the region's precious topsoil, twice as much earth in one afternoon than had been excavated during the seven-year construction of the Panama Canal.

Above: Before he and all those around him were plunged into darkness by the unprecedented storm, a photographer was able to take this picture of the extraordinary wall of dust that engulfed the southern plains on Black Sunday.

Opposite: After she took this photograph on Black Sunday, photographer Dorothea Lange wrote, "It was conditions of this sort which forced many farmers to abandon the area."

Covered in Dust

It would become known as "Black Sunday" and out of the same storm another name would emerge. As he traveled the area in order to write about the extraordinary effects of the storm, Associated Press reporter Robert Geiger created the term "dust bowl" to describe what the region had become. Tragically, for those who lived there, it was the most appropriate name that could have been invented.

Texas judge Wilson Cowen wrote, "The dust was deposited clear up to the windowsills in these farmhouses. . . . And even about half of the front door was blocked by this sand. And if people inside wanted to get out, they had to climb out through the window to get out with a shovel to shovel out the front door. . . . There was no longer any yard at all, there was not a green sprig, not a living thing of any kind, not even a field mouse. Nothing."

Ernie Pyle, a reporter who would become one of the nation's most famous journalists, put it even more simply after visiting the region. "If you would like to have your heart broken, just come out here," he wrote. "This is the dust-storm country. It is the saddest land I have ever seen."

And the dust, the sand, the dirt—whatever it was called—kept on coming. One of the most popular stories of the time was that of the tourist from the East who asked a Kansas wheat farmer where he could find the Dust Bowl. The farmer's answer was simple. "Just stay where you are," he told the tourist, "and it'll come to you."

Above: *For many who saw it, this photograph told it all. The dust storms had completely buried and destroyed this farm vehicle while turning 100 million acres of the nation's most valuable soil into a vast desert.*

Opposite: *Photographer Arthur Rothstein had a hard time getting close enough to capture this image of dust-buried buildings on an Oklahoma farm.*

An Agonizing Decision

"We are getting deeper and deeper in dust." —THE BOISE CITY NEWS

More than ever, the people of the Dust Bowl found themselves struggling to cope with the way the dust had a part in every aspect of their lives. "All we could do about it," recalled a Kansas woman, "was just sit in our dusty chairs, gaze at each other through the fog that filled the room and watch that fog settle slowly and silently, covering everything—including ourselves—in a thick, brownish gray blanket. . . . It got into cupboards and clothes closets; our faces were as dirty as if we had rolled in the dirt; our hair was gray and stiff and we ground dirt between our teeth."

But, difficult as it was, coping with the dust in the house or on the highway was nothing compared to trying to cope with what the dust storms had done to the crops. "When I knew that my crop was irrevocably gone I experienced a deathly feeling which, I hope, can affect a man only once in a lifetime," wrote Lawrence Svobida. "My dreams and ambitions had been flouted by nature, and my shattered ideals seemed gone forever. The very desire to make a success of my life was gone; the spirit and urge to strive were dead within me. Fate had dealt me a cruel blow above which I felt utterly unable to rise."

He was not alone. Hundreds of thousands whose crops had been destroyed—out of money and with no prospect of making any in the foreseeable future—were faced with the most agonizing decision of their lives. Should they abandon the land that had been so good to them for so long, land that in most cases had been in their family for generations? Or should they stay, hoping that things would get better?

Above: *The photographer's caption for this picture in Salisaw, Oklahoma, read, "Drought farmers line the shady side of the main street of the town while their crops burn up in the fields."*

Opposite: *For many Dust Bowl families the determining factor in whether to stay or leave had to do with concern for their children. Would there be any future for them in a land that had turned to dust?*

The Art of Photography

"Photography is a way of feeling, of touching, of loving. What you have caught on film is captured forever . . . it remembers little things, long after you have forgotten everything."
—PHOTOGRAPHER AARON SISKIND

When photography (which literally means "writing with light") was first introduced in 1839 by the Frenchman Louis Daguerre, it was regarded as a miracle. People were astounded that they could possess exact likenesses of themselves, their relatives, and their friends. Not only that, but for the first time in history they could see what the celebrities of their day really looked like.

What was equally amazing was how quickly technical advancements were made that put picture-taking in the hands of the average person. The first cameras were extremely cumbersome and produced images that could not be reproduced. Even after cameras were invented that made it possible to make a limitless number of copies of each picture taken, the glass plates that were used as negatives were fragile and difficult to manage. When George Eastman introduced the world to a relatively small, easy-to-use, inexpensive camera that used film instead of glass plates in 1888, photography truly came of age.

When the first dust storms hit the southern plains in 1931, photography was still less than one hundred years old. By this time, professional and amateur photographers were pursuing a variety of approaches within the medium. Many were concentrating on taking portraits, which, until more sophisticated cameras were invented, had been the main photographic approach. Others, called "landscape photographers," were training their cameras on the extraordinarily varied American terrain. Still others were following in the footsteps of earlier men and women who, by producing photographs that rivaled paintings in both beauty and creativity, had gained photography acceptance as a true art form. And, by the 1930s, there was yet another photographic approach, one that in many ways had captured the public's attention most of all. It was called "documentary photography," and throughout the thirties, the photographers who captured thousands of pictures of the Dust Bowl and its victims would raise the genre to its greatest heights.

Above: *This daguerreotype self-portrait, taken by Robert Cornelius in 1839, is the earliest surviving American photograph.*

Opposite: *The 1930s were a unique time. The people of the Dust Bowl were a unique breed of people. And it is through the power of photography that they will best be remembered.*

Heroes of the Dust Bowl

O you daughters of the West!
O you young and elder daughters! O you mothers and you wives!
Never must you be divided, in our ranks you move united.
—WALT WHITMAN, "PIONEERS! O PIONEERS!"

From the time that the Great Plains had been settled, it was the women who had carried the heaviest load. And, like those who had come before them, it was the women who would be the real heroes of the Dust Bowl. Mothers, wives, nurses, cooks, full partners with their husbands in running the family farm, the Dust Bowl women were all these and more. For, in the face of seeing their family's lives ruined by dust, in most cases they would somehow manage to see to it that the family survived and stayed together. And, in most cases, they would make the agonizing decision as to whether to flee from their dust-covered homes.

Some, however, like Nettie Featherston (opposite), had no choice. They had become so poor that they had no means to leave. "The worst thing we did was when we sold the car, but we had to sell it to eat," she told Dorothea Lange. Later, she stated, "We lived in a little two-room house. Had a wood stove that we cooked blackeye peas on. We ate so many blackeye peas that I never wanted to see another one. . . . Your kids would cry for something to eat and you couldn't get it. I just prayed and prayed and prayed all the time that God would take care of us and not let my children starve. All our people left here. . . . But we were so poor that we couldn't have went to California or nowhere else."

Dorothea Lange, who photographed hundreds of these women, was so taken with their strength and determination that she wrote: "These are women of the American soil. They are a hardy stock. They are of the roots of our country. . . . They are not our well-advertised women of beauty and fashion. . . . These women represent a different mode of life. They are *of themselves* a very great American style."

Above: *For most women of the vast plains, the greatest challenge of all, even in good times, was combating the loneliness that came from living miles away from their nearest neighbor.*

Opposite: *Dorothea Lange titled this photograph of Nettie Featherston "Woman of the High Plains." Asked to explain how she found the determination to face each day, Featherston replied, "If you die, you're dead, that's all."*

The Great Depression

The Dust Bowl disaster was not the only tragedy to strike the United States. At the same time, the rest of the nation was suffering from a different type of calamity. As late as 1928, when the farmers of the southern plains were thriving, most of the rest of the country was prospering as well. So much so that President Herbert Hoover would proclaim, "We shall soon . . . be in sight of the day when poverty will be banished from this nation."

He could not have been more wrong. Just one year later, in 1929, beginning with the collapse of the stock market, the entire American economy collapsed. As thousands of banks failed, millions of people lost their life savings. Many lost their homes. By 1931, some twelve million Americans had lost their jobs. It was called the Great Depression, the greatest economic disaster in the nation's history.

It was a time of enormous hardship, one that would not end until America's entry into World War II in 1941. Almost everyone was affected, including the nation's young people—who, like their parents, found their lives drastically changed.

"I remember all of a sudden we had to move," a Cleveland youngster recalled. "My father lost his job and we moved into a . . . garage. . . . It was awfully cold when you opened those garage doors. We would sleep with rugs and blankets over the top of us and we would dress under the sheets. . . . My father owned three or four houses. . . . But he lost these one by one."

A Texas youngster had his own recollections. "We tried hard enough, and everybody did their best. Marie made the swellest wax flowers. . . . Mother tried to sell some home made baked goods. And Dad did everything. We did our best . . . but . . . nobody had any money."

Above: *The expressions on the faces of this mother and her two children dramatically reveal how they have been affected by the Great Depression.*

Opposite: *Just as Dorothea Lange's "Migrant Mother" photograph became a symbol of the Dust Bowl experience, this picture she took on "skid row" in San Francisco became regarded by many as a dramatic symbol of the Great Depression.*

Champion of Recovery

His name was Franklin Delano Roosevelt and he was a most unlikely champion of the poor. Born to great wealth, he had enjoyed a financially privileged life before being elected president of the United States. Yet in a speech before Congress, he would declare, "The test of our progress is not whether we add more to the abundance of those who have much; it is whether we provide enough for those who have too little."

By becoming the nation's leader during the early stages of both the Great Depression and the Dust Bowl disaster, Roosevelt took on one of the greatest challenges that any American president had faced since Abraham Lincoln carried the burden of saving the Union during the Civil War. Roosevelt soon proved that he was up to the task.

Realizing that his first priority had to be calming the fears of millions caught up in hard times, he began his first inaugural address by promising that "this great Nation will endure as it has endured, will revive and will prosper." He then backed up this pledge by creating a host of what he called "New Deal" agencies, designed to give work to the unemployed and to bring about economic recovery. Among these many agencies were the Works Progress Administration (WPA), the Farm Security Administration (FSA), the Civilian Conservation Corps (CCC), and the National Recovery Administration (NRA). Because these and the other new relief organizations were commonly referred to by their initials, they became known as Roosevelt's "alphabet agencies."

From the time he took office, one of Roosevelt's most often expressed beliefs was that economic recovery would not take place until farmers stopped destroying their land and prosperity returned to the American farm. Stating that "the Nation that destroys its soil destroys itself," he made certain that many of his reform and relief programs were aimed at the farmers, programs that would eventually be of great benefit to the Dust Bowl victims.

Above: *Artist Norman Rockwell's "Four Freedoms" posters were inspired by a speech that President Franklin Roosevelt gave to Congress.*

Opposite: *President Franklin D. Roosevelt signs one of the hundreds of pieces of legislation he initiated. In Roosevelt, a poverty-stricken nation found a leader committed to helping the poor and the unemployed.*

The WPA

"I had been out of work for almost a year. The WPA not only gave me a job. It gave me back my dignity." —NEW YORK RESIDENT SHERMAN BERGER

In 1935, Roosevelt created the Works Progress Administration (WPA), the most far-reaching of the New Deal agencies, to provide work for as many of the nation's unemployed as possible.

Over the next eight years, the WPA would not only put almost nine million people to work, it would literally change the face of the nation. The variety of the more than 1.4 million projects that the agency sponsored was astounding. They ranged from the building of schools, libraries, fire stations, and other public buildings to the production of plays, operas, and musicals; from the construction of dams and bridges to teaching illiterate adults to read and write; from the creation of state guides and folk life compilations to the building of roads and airports.

Among those to whom the WPA gave employment were hundreds of photographers who, like the nation's artists and writers, had been particularly hard hit by the Great Depression. In fact, without government help, many questioned whether the arts in America would survive. Included in the ranks of WPA photographers were such talented men and women as Berenice Abbott, Edward Weston, Minor White, Sonya Noskowiak, Nacho Bravo, and Arnold Eagle.

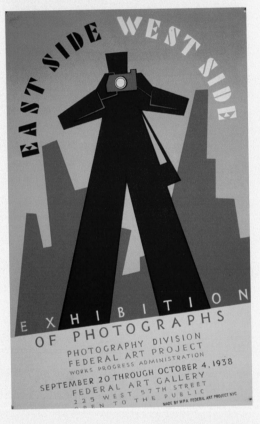

These photographers, like their fellow creative artists, were extremely grateful for the opportunity the WPA gave them to remain working in their profession during the hardest of times. As Arnold Eagle stated, "[There] always was a feeling of service, a desire to give back something for the relief that had been offered." The photographers and other WPA artists not only "gave back," they made so many advancements in each of their disciplines that by the time they were through, they would bring about nothing less than what *Fortune* magazine called "a cultural revolution in America."

Above: *By presenting nationwide exhibitions of the work of its talented photographers, the WPA introduced millions of Americans to masterful photography.*

Opposite: *Of all the government agencies created during the Great Depression, the WPA put the largest number of people to work. These workers are painting a section of one of the many dams the WPA built.*

Documentary Photography

"**There were two things** I wanted to do," photographer Lewis Hine stated in 1939. "I wanted to show the things that had to be corrected; I wanted to show the things that had to be appreciated." More than seventy years later, Hine's statement still stands as a most effective explanation of what documentary photography is all about.

Almost from the time that the first pictures were taken, it became obvious that photographs could both reveal and persuade in ways that had never been possible before. As early as the 1880s, for example, Solomon Butcher, determined to visually record pioneer families and their sod houses before they disappeared forever, took thousands of photographs of these people and their earthen dwellings. Some twenty years later, Edward Curtis began what would be a thirty-year project photographing every Native American tribe he could reach before their way of life also vanished.

During the same era, other pioneering documentary photographers were taking pictures of "things that had to be corrected." Among them were Jacob Riis, whose pictures of the horrendous conditions under which millions of European immigrants to New York were forced to live led to the cleaning up of the New York slums, and Lewis Hine, whose photographs of tens of thousands of children working in the nation's factories and mines led to the passage of the nation's first child-labor laws.

It would be the photographs taken by the Dust Bowl photographers, however, that would capture the attention of the American public as no other images had ever done. By the end of the 1930s, these pictures would establish photography as the universal language, understood by people everywhere, and recognized as one of the greatest forms of communication the world had ever known.

Above: *It was with pictures such as this one, of children working from dawn to dusk operating dangerous textile machines, that Lewis Hine pioneered the field of documentary photography and played a major role in abolishing child labor in America.*

Opposite: *Documentary photography reveals a time, a place, and a people and preserves it forever. The best documentary photography also makes us care about the people being portrayed.*

Portraying a Nation in Hard Times

"We just took pictures that cried out to be taken." —FSA PHOTOGRAPHER BEN SHAHN

In the same year that the WPA was created, another important government relief agency began its work. Called the Farm Security Administration (FSA), its purpose was to give aid to the nation's farmers. In order to document the FSA's activities, a special photographic division titled the Historical Section was created. What no one could have imagined was that this section would produce photographs so powerful and influential that they would eventually help to bring aid to those caught up in the Dust Bowl tragedy.

The person named to head the FSA Historical Section was Roy Stryker, who began by hiring some of the nation's most talented photographers—men and women he knew to be as socially committed as they were expert with a camera. Among them were such future giants of photography as Walker Evans, Ben Shahn, Carl Mydans, Dorothea Lange, Arthur Rothstein, Marion Post Wolcott, John Vachon, Jack Delano, Russell Lee, and Gordon Parks.

From the beginning, Stryker realized that with such photographic talent and government support and funding at his disposal he had a unique opportunity. Along with having his photographers capture images of FSA agents helping people cope with hard times, he could have them capture nothing less than a portrayal of a people and a nation. Even more important, he could have them record what to him was the greatest lesson provided by those caught up in the Great Depression, particularly the Dust Bowl victims—the dignity of the human spirit in the face of adversity.

Above: *It was photographs like this that made Roy Stryker proclaim of the pictures his photographers took, "Dignity versus despair. . . . I believe that dignity wins out."*

Opposite: *FSA photographer John Vachon's picture of the children of a farmer who was struggling to make ends meet in the Great Depression is regarded by many photographic historians as one of the most touching photographs ever taken.*

Taking America's Portrait

"You're having a tough time here and the rest of the country needs to see pictures of it so that they can appreciate what you're going through." —RUSSELL LEE TO THE DUST BOWL VICTIMS WHOSE PHOTOGRAPHS HE TOOK

The FSA photographers took their pictures at a time when, as historian Irving Bernstein stated, "The anguish of the American people . . . demanded a pictorial record." And of all the more than 270,000 photographs that were taken, the most memorable of all would be the images of the Dust Bowl victims.

Among those men and women who documented the Dust Bowl experience was Russell Lee, who, of all the FSA photographers, created the largest body of work and covered the greatest geographic territory. Lee continually crisscrossed the country, creating a visual documentation that earned him the title "the man who created America's portrait." But it was the Dust Bowl victims he encountered, particularly in Texas, Oklahoma, and New Mexico, who most captured his emotions. Aware of the magnitude of what was taking place and the importance of his pictures, he often took many photographs of the same subject, determined to capture the mood of the people in front of his lens while at the same time portraying their humanity. As Lee's fellow photographer Ave Bonar stated, "He gave me an appreciation for respecting people when photographing them."

Lee was not only the FSA's most prolific and well-traveled photographer, he was also arguably its most innovative. His development of a multiple-flash attachment to his camera enabled him to produce interior photographs, such as the one on this page, that were far clearer and more detailed than most other indoor photographs of his day.

Above: *Pictures such as this one have led University of Texas photographic historian Linda Peterson to proclaim that "[Russell Lee's] essential compassion for the human condition shines forth in every image."*

Opposite: *Lee was one of the few photographers on hand when the great westward migration began, enabling him to take pictures like this one of a Dust Bowl wife and mother packing as many provisions into the family car as possible for the long journey to California.*

The Great Escape

"The land just blew away. We had to go somewhere." —KANSAS PREACHER

The Flight From the Dust Bowl was the largest migration in American history. By the end of the 1930s, some 2.5 million people had moved out of the southern plains. Some headed for states just outside the Dust Bowl area. Others made states such as Arizona and New Mexico their destination. The majority, however—more than 200,000—were determined to reach California.

There were several reasons why so many chose to seek a better life there. California's mild climate was particularly attractive to people whose lives had been completely overturned by the harsh natural conditions of the plains. This mild climate provided one of the longest growing seasons in the nation and a wide variety of crops, giving the migrants hope that they would be able to find work harvesting these crops throughout the year. Many of the dispossessed had, in fact, read advertisements placed by California fruit and vegetable growers heralding the

bounty of that state's crops and the need for people to cultivate and pick them. If they had to make so drastic a move, at least they would be taking on work with which they were familiar.

This far westward flight was also motivated by the fact that, at a time when the nation's highway system was far from having been developed, there was one great road that led directly to California. It was officially named "Route 66," but before the Dust Bowl migrant experience was over it would become known in song, story, and legend as "the Mother Road."

The most clearly stated reasons for heading so far from home could be found in the migrants' own words. "I'm going west because this country's through," stated one Oklahoman. "There isn't anything here for anyone."

Above: *A couple begins to pitch the tent in which they will sleep every evening of their long journey to California. In all probability, the same tent served as their living quarters once they reached their destination.*

Opposite: *By the mid 1930s, scenes such as this one were commonplace on every road leading from the southern plains to California—vehicle after vehicle of desperate people, driven from the land they had long called home.*

The Endless Road

"People have been leaving the Great Plains by tens of thousands every year. To me, that is the real tragedy of the Dust Bowl." —KANSAS FARMER LAWRENCE SVOBIDA

"We're bound for . . . Lubbock, [Texas,] . . . but we'll be in California yet. We're not going back . . . [I] believe I can better myself," one Arkansan stated. It was a determination and spirit shared by hundreds of thousands of those who traveled into the unknown, heading halfway across the continent never really knowing whether they would be able to complete the trip or what they would find at journey's end. The roads over which they traveled were foreboding in themselves, seemingly stretching on forever. Most of the migrants had never been out of their state, let alone their region. Now most were embarking on the longest journey of their lives, one that, only a relatively short time before, none could have imagined they would be compelled to take.

By far, the vast majority of pictures that photographers took of the Dust Bowl experience were images of the men, women, and children who were at the center of the tragic development. But some of the most powerful photographs, like those that revealed how the dust storms transformed the land, had no people in them at all. One of the most haunting of all these peopleless images is the photograph on the opposite page, depicting one of the seemingly endless roads over which the migrants would be forced to travel. Commenting on the picture and what it evokes, author/sociologist Robert Coles wrote, "On the day . . . when Dorothea Lange photographed the road, and called it 'Migrant Route,' there was not a soul upon it . . . , yet it is packed with presences, crowded, we sense, with hundreds upon hundreds of thousands of men, women, and children . . . driven to take this road."

Above: *Almost no family was able to make the trip to California without experiencing some sort of car trouble. Here, a woman gazes off in the distance while the broken-down automobile is being repaired.*

Opposite: *Long after their Dust Bowl exodus was over, many of the migrants would describe their journey over mile after mile of never-ending highway running through totally barren land as one of the most difficult experiences of their lives.*

Journey to the Unknown

"It's a very difficult thing to be exposed to the new and strange worlds that you know nothing about and find your way. . . . It's a hard thing to be lost." —DOROTHEA LANGE

Some 200,000 Dust Bowl victims took to the road. Terribly poor, they sold everything they could to buy an old truck or car, known in those days as jalopies. Then they packed whatever they could— mattresses, chairs, prized possessions—into the vehicles, often tying them down to the sides or the roofs. They knew that it would be a long, arduous journey. For most it turned out to be far more difficult than they could have imagined.

If they had been making the more-than-1,500-mile trip in relatively new cars or trucks, the long distance and the road conditions would still have taken their toll on the vehicles. But most were traveling in cars or trucks that had seen better days. All along the way, vehicles broke down. Then members of the family would have to hitch a ride into the nearest town, hoping to find work that would pay them enough to purchase whatever replacement part was needed. Even if by some miracle their vehicle did not break down, most migrants still had to periodically stop and find work in order to buy more food and gasoline.

But most of all, the trip was made extraordinarily difficult by the situation in which the migrants found themselves. They had been forced off their land. They were far from certain that they could complete their journey. They had no idea what really awaited them when they reached California.

Above: *The caption that Dorothea Lange wrote to accompany this picture read, "Stalled on the desert, facing a future in California. No money, ten children."*

Opposite: *The caption to this photograph read, "More Oklahomans reach California via the cotton fields of Arizona." According to the caption, one of those in the car stated simply, "We got blowed out of Oklahoma."*

Reformer with a Camera

"You put a camera around your neck in the morning . . . and there it is, an appendage . . . that shares your life with you. The camera is an instrument that teaches people how to see without a camera." —DOROTHEA LANGE

By the time legions of Dust Bowl refugees took to the road and headed out of the stricken region, FSA photographers were at work, ready to record the migrants' flight. The vast majority of these pictures were taken by a woman destined to become one of the world's most famous photographers. Born in Hoboken, New Jersey, Dorothea Lange began her career as a portrait photographer, first in New York City and then in San Francisco. When the Great Depression began, Lange abandoned her portrait work and took to the streets, where she photographed the plight of San Franciscans who had lost their jobs. Her powerful and sensitive images of the unemployed and homeless caught the attention of Roy Stryker, who asked her to come join the FSA photographic corps.

From the moment she began capturing her images of the Dust Bowl victims, Lange was taken with the courage displayed by those who had been driven from their land and faced an unknown future. "Their roots were all torn out," she wrote. "The only background they had was a background of utter poverty. . . . I had to get my camera to register the things about those people that were more important than how poor they were—their pride, their strength, their spirit."

Accused by some of being too much a propagandist by using her photographs to influence the opinions of others, she had a simple reply. "Everything," she said, "is propaganda for what you believe in. . . . The harder and the more deeply you believe in anything, the more in a sense you're a propagandist. . . . I never have been able to come to the conclusion that that's a bad word." Thanks to this conviction and the sensitive way she portrayed the Dust Bowl victims, Dorothea Lange earned the title "the supreme humanist."

Above: *Above all else, Dorothea Lange's photographs of Dust Bowl victims reflect her desire to portray their humanity and pride, no matter how dire their circumstances.*

Opposite: *Dorothea Lange sits atop the car she used to follow the Dust Bowl migrants. Her camera seems terribly large to us today, but it was much easier to handle than the far more cumbersome cameras that were common only a decade earlier.*

An Important Book

"Because they were all lonely and perplexed, because they had all come from a place of sadness and worry and defeat, and because they were all going to a new mysterious place, they huddled together." —JOHN STEINBECK, *THE GRAPES OF WRATH*

From the moment that Dorothea Lange encountered the Dust Bowl migrants, she felt compelled to make the whole nation aware of what these people were going through. The photographs she produced were so powerful that they, in turn, inspired others to make the migrants' condition known. Among them was the famed American author John Steinbeck. After viewing many of the images, Steinbeck was so moved that he wrote a novel he titled *The Grapes of Wrath*, portraying the migrants' plight in words as eloquent as Lange's pictures.

"And then the dispossessed were drawn west—," Steinbeck wrote, "from Kansas, Oklahoma, Texas, New Mexico; . . . families, . . . dusted out. . . . Car-loads, caravans, homeless and hungry; twenty thousand and fifty thousand and a hundred thousand and two hundred thousand. They streamed over the mountains, hungry and restless—restless as ants, scurrying to find work to do—to lift, to push, to pick, to cut—anything, any burden to bear, for food. The kids are hungry. We got no place to live. Like ants scurrying for work, for food, and most of all for land."

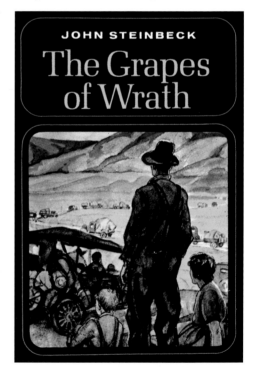

From the time it was published in 1939, *The Grapes of Wrath* became one of the most widely read books in America. Commenting on the enormous impact that it had on the public, scholar John Timmerman wrote, "*The Grapes of Wrath* may well be the most thoroughly discussed novel . . . of twentieth century American literature." As Steinbeck did in his book, Dorothea Lange also revealed how the Dust Bowl migrants often sought comfort in each other. The photograph opposite, showing families huddled together under a billboard advertising the comforts of traveling by train, was one that Lange was compelled to take. Traveling in that fashion was the last thing that road-weary migrants could afford.

Above: The Grapes of Wrath *is one of the most honored books of all time, awarded both the Pulitzer Prize and the Nobel Prize for Literature.*

Opposite: *"In the daylight," John Steinbeck wrote in* The Grapes of Wrath, *"[the migrants] scuttled like bugs to the westward; and as the dark caught them, they clustered like bugs near to shelter and to water."*

Arriving in California

Whether it took a few weeks or as much as six months, somehow most of those who set out for California, like the family on the opposite page, made it there. But their troubles were far from over. For what they discovered was that California was not the Promised Land they had hoped it would be.

The weather was certainly beautiful, and the fields were filled with a greater abundance and variety of crops than they could have imagined. But California, like the rest of the nation, was feeling the effects of the Great Depression. Many of its own citizens, having lost their jobs, had been forced to take on work in the fields. From the moment they arrived, the Dust Bowl refugees were looked upon as a threat to these workers, who were desperate to earn whatever money they could.

The result was that, after enduring the incredible hardships of their long journey, the Dust Bowlers were made aware they were not welcome in the place upon which they had put all their hopes. Some were even given a difficult time before they actually set foot on California soil. A writer for *Collier's*, one of the nation's most popular magazines, witnessed what took place when one exhausted family reached the California border and was confronted by a state trooper.

"Very erect and primly severe," the reporter wrote, "[the trooper] addressed the slumped driver of a rolling wreck that screamed from every hinge, bearing and coupling. 'California's . . . overcrowded now. No use to come farther,' [the trooper] cried. The half-collapsed driver ignored him—merely turned his head to be sure his numerous family was still with him. They were so tightly wedged in, that escape was impossible. . . . And the forlorn man on the moaning car looked at him, dull, emotionless, incredibly weary, and said, 'So? Well, you ought to see what they got where I come from.'"

Above: *The photographer's caption for this photograph read, "Children of Oklahoma drought refugee in . . . California." What it couldn't reveal is what they were thinking about now that they were about to live in a strange place hundreds of miles from home.*

Opposite: *Members of a Dust Bowl family, having made it successfully past California border guards, pause to consider their circumstances. They have reached the land of sunshine and palm trees, but will they be able to find enough work to maintain themselves?*

In the Fields

"If you lose your pluck you lose the most there is in you—all you've got to live with."
—EIGHTY-YEAR-OLD DUST BOWL MIGRANT

The migrants were tired, they were hungry, and they were unwelcome. And because their vehicles were so battered and they themselves were so bedraggled from both their circumstances and their long journey, they were also scorned. They had come from several Dust Bowl states other than Oklahoma, but they would all be called "Okies" by the Californians. They were labeled "shiftless" and "ignorant," and were accused of stealing jobs from the native population. They would continually hear cries of "Okies, go home!" or would encounter signs that read No Okies Allowed.

But they had already lost so much. They had traveled so far. And they had nowhere else to go. They could not allow themselves to be defeated.

Penniless, many of the migrants pitched tents, often along irrigation ditches where at least they would have water available to them. Many others, after scrounging for scrap wood and metal, discarded canvas, and anything else they could find, literally threw together makeshift dwellings like the one on the opposite page. Then they went looking for work in the fields. Aware of the Dust Bowlers' desperation, crop owners offered them extremely low wages for back-breaking work. The migrants had no choice but to accept them. "We come from all states and we can't make a dollar a day in this field noways," the man hauling the crate of newly picked carrots in the photograph on this page told the photographer. "Working from seven in the morning till twelve noon we earn an average of thirty five cents."

Above: *Despite their willingness to work as many hours in the fields as possible, the low wages they received destroyed the hopes of most migrants that life would be better in California.*

Opposite: *According to the caption that Dorothea Lange wrote for this photograph, these Dust Bowl children were now living in "one of the largest [pea-picking] camps in California."*

A Special Tragedy

"If you are the kind of [person] who likes to say 'Am I my brother's keeper?', don't look at these pictures—they may change your mind." —PHOTOGRAPHER EDWARD STEICHEN

With such low wages, every member of a migrant family was forced to work in the fields—even the young children. For them, there would be no time for school or for play. Instead, if the family was lucky enough to find work, they reported to the fields at dawn and then spent hours in the broiling sun either painfully stooped over or on their hands and knees picking various types of crops.

For many of these children's parents, the sight of their youngsters performing such laborious work was the most devastating evidence of how dramatically their fortunes had changed since they had become the victims of drought and wind and dust. "Leaving everything we had known behind had been hard enough," Lillian Berger wrote in a letter to friends back in Texas, "but watching the children who had been so happy back home work their fingers to the bone was almost more than we could bear."

Those FSA photographers who followed the migrants to California, such as Dorothea Lange and Russell Lee, shared the parents' anguish. But in their desire to bring aid to the Dust Bowlers, as well as chronicle their experiences, they also saw the opportunity to produce some of the most poignant of all their pictures. The photograph on the opposite page is a prime example. Who could not help but be moved by the image of the very young girl standing sad and barely awake at seven in the morning waiting to be driven to the fields? And who could fail to notice the enormous sack in her hands that she would be required to fill several times with carrots or peas or beans or some other crop before her day was over?

Above: *A young migrant from Oklahoma pauses briefly from his pea-picking work. The photographer's caption for this picture reveals that he began each day's work at 5 a.m.*

Opposite: *When famous American photographer Ansel Adams was shown pictures such as this one, he told Roy Stryker, "What you've got are not photographers. They're a bunch of sociologists with cameras."*

Following the Crops

"You can make it here if you sleep late and eat little, but it's pretty tough—there's so many people." —UNIDENTIFIED TEXAS MIGRANT FARMER

The Dust Bowl refugees not only had to endure the hardships of toiling in the California fields, but, in order to survive, they had to follow the harvest around the state. When oranges were ready to be picked they had to travel to wherever the groves were located. When it came time for the pea harvest, they had to get back in their cars and trucks and journey miles to where the peas were grown. The same was true of carrots, lemons, cotton, and all the other crops.

The experiences of the woman in the photograph on the opposite page were typical of so many of those who had fled from the dust. The caption that the photographer supplied with the picture read: "Had fifty dollars when set out. Went to Phoenix, picked cotton . . . made eighty cents a day. . . . Stayed until school closed. Went to Idaho, picked peas until August. Left McCall with forty dollars 'in hand.' Went to Cedar City and Parawon, Utah, a distance of 700 miles. Picked peas through September. Went to Hollister, California. Picked peas through October. Left Hollister for Calipatria [California] for early peas which froze."

The caption then quoted the woman as stating, "Back in Oklahoma we are sinking. You work your head off for a crop and then see it burn up. You live in debts that you can never get out of. This isn't a good life, but I say it's a better life than it was."

It may have seemed to be a better life than it had been covered with dust, but was it really? Some migrants began to wonder. Dust Bowler Mildred Lenora Morris Ward stated, "I thought that it would be so easy to work. All you had to do was just go and ask for it, and you'd get the work. I didn't realize what it was really like. . . . [In Oklahoma] we were kind a looked up to and at least respected. [Then to] come out here to this, where we were nothing."

Above: *The Dust Bowl refugees followed the crops in almost every type of vehicle imaginable, bringing their children along to aid them in their labors.*

Opposite: *The photographer's caption revealed that despite the great distances she had already traveled to obtain work, this woman was now waiting to hear where the next crops were ready to be picked.*

Stories in Pictures: The Photo-Essay

> *"To see life; to see the world; to eyewitness great events; to watch the faces of the poor and the gestures of the proud."* —CREDO FOR *LIFE* MAGAZINE

Over the course of its hundred-year history, photography became both the world's universal language and one of its greatest sources of information. By the mid-1930s, in the midst of the Dust Bowl crisis, a new development had taken place as magazine and newspaper editors discovered that readers were particularly captivated when a series of photographs dealing with a specific subject were printed together to tell a story in pictures. This new approach came to be called the "photo-essay," and it revolutionized the world of photography.

The photographers who produced photo-essays were called "photojournalists" and many of them would create their stories in pictures for a magazine called *Life,* which, after being launched in 1936, became the most widely read magazine of its day. A year later, another major picture magazine, called *Look,* was founded. Together, these two publications brought photographs into the homes of millions of people around the world and established the photo-essay as one of the principal means of conveying human conditions and global developments.

Although none of the FSA Dust Bowl photographers deliberately created photographic essays for the agency, by the end of the 1930s, *Life, Look,* and other publications were putting together picture stories based on their photographs. The opposite page shows a spread that was part of a long photo-essay titled "Why John Steinbeck Wrote *The Grapes of Wrath.*" The photograph on this page was part of a *Look* photo-essay titled "Caravans of Hunger: Thousands of Farmers Wander California's Highways."

Above: *Even though a photo-essay is made up of several pictures telling a story, each image, like this one in a* Look *picture story on migrants looking for work in California, has to be able to stand on its own as a powerful visual statement.*

Opposite: *Since so many people had read* The Grapes of Wrath, *John Steinbeck's novel of the Dust Bowl experience, this photo-essay became one of the most popular of all* Look's *picture stories.*

AMERICA'S REFUGEES . . . Continued

Why John Steinbeck Wrote "The Grapes of Wrath"

JOHN STEINBECK, 37-year-old Californian, has lived among the American farm families which fled to California from depression and dust and remained to become migrant harvesters of its crops. He knows their wretched living conditions, the organized oppression they meet, their grim tenacity in the face of hunger and disease. He tells their story in his novel, "The Grapes of Wrath," from which are taken in Steinbeck's own words the captions for these pictures by staff photographers of LOOK and the federal Farm Securities Administration.

In the Water-Cut Gullies the earth dusted down in dry little streams. Gophers and ant lions started small avalanches . . . "God knows the lan' ain't no good . . . but it's our land. We measured it and broke it up. We were born on it . . . died on it. Even if it's no good, it's still ours. That's what makes it ours—being born on it, working it, dying on it. That makes ownership, not a paper with numbers on it."

The Houses Were Left Vacant on the land, and the land was vacant because of this . . . The tenant system won't work any more. One man on a tractor can take the place of 12 or 14 families. Pay him a wage and take all the crop. . . . "It's dirt hard for folks to tear up an' go. Folks like us . . . We ain't shif'less. Till we got tractored off, we was people with a farm."

Cars Limping Along Highway 66 . . . cutdown cars full a stoves an' pans an' mattresses an' kids an' chickens . . . "F we can on'y get to California before this ol' jug blows up."

Eighty Cents a Hundred first time over the field . . . 90 cents second time over . . . "They say a thousan' men are on the way to this cotton field. We'll be fightin' for a row tomorra" . . .

And every day they went into the fields and picked the cotton, and every night they had meat . . . "Wisht it would last. It ain't much money, God knows, but I wisht it would last."

And Then the Raids—the swoop of armed deputies on the squatters' camps . . . "Get out . . . We got orders to get you out of here . . . We don't want you Okies settlin' down."

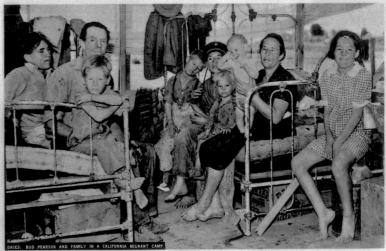

OKIES: BUD PEARSON AND FAMILY IN A CALIFORNIA MIGRANT CAMP

"I Can't Tell Ya about them little fellas layin' in the tent with their bellies puffed out an' jus' skin on their bones, an' shiverin' an' whinin' like pups, an' me runnin' aroun' tryin' to get work—not for money, not for wages! Jus' for a cup a flour an' a spoon a lard. Know what we et all week? Biled nettles an' fried dough! . . . Tent ain't gonna be nice in the winter . . . Gotta have a house when the rains come . . . I tell ya we got to . . . Jus' so's it's got a roof an' a floor. Jus' to keep the little fellas off'n the groun'." **Continued on Next Page**

Help at Last

"I see a United States which can demonstrate that, under democratic methods of government, ... the lowest standard of living can be raised far above the level of mere subsistence."
—PRESIDENT FRANKLIN D. ROOSEVELT, SECOND INAUGURAL ADDRESS

The migrants had removed themselves from one desperate situation in the Dust Bowl to another in California. But in the late 1930s, their fortunes began to change. Thanks in no small measure to the haunting images of them both on the road and in California, the government began to take action.

In 1937, the federal government began to build cleaner and better camps for migrants. By the end of that year, seven of these camps were operating in California's San Joaquin Valley alone. These federal facilities were clean and had showers and bathrooms. They also had auditoriums and recreation halls where the migrants could gather together and find enjoyment. Equally important, the government gave the migrants the opportunity to elect people from their ranks to help run the camps and plan activities. By 1941, tens of thousands of Dust Bowl refugees had moved into these camps, which gave them a sense of dignity, community, and, at last, hope.

In a vital development, the United States government also began granting relief checks to tens of thousands of the migrants, aid that literally helped them survive. Inspired by the federal government's actions, the California state government instituted programs of its own designed to improve the migrant families' condition. Included were nursery schools, special education opportunities for older youngsters, and visiting nurse programs.

The final step in the migrants' reversal of fortune came not through federal or state aid but through the events of history. In 1941, the United States entered World War II. In California, as in the rest of the nation, the economy

dramatically improved as billions of dollars were poured into the defense industry. Many of the migrants went off to fight in the war. Those who remained behind—both women and men—found jobs in West Coast shipyards, aircraft factories, and other defense plants, where they received a higher wage than most had ever earned. When the war ended in 1945, thousands of the former Dust Bowlers remained in California and other West Coast states and took part in the enormous postwar growth of that section of the country.

Above: *The living facilities at the camps that the government built for the migrants were a far cry from what the Dust Bowl refugees had previously experienced in California.*

Opposite: *Included among the activities at the government-built migrant camps were many created for young people. Here, children at the Shafter, California, camp pose for the camera during a Halloween party.*

Poet of the Dust Bowl

"Left Oklahoma and went out to west Texas . . . right square in the big middle of the dust bowl. That's where the wheat grows. . . . Where the dust blows. And the farmer owes."
—WOODY GUTHRIE

"Songs," wrote **John Steinbeck**, "are the statements of a people. You can learn more about people by listening to their songs than in any other way, for into the songs go all the hopes and hurts, the angers, fears, the wants and aspirations." The Dust Bowl tragedy inspired many songs, many written by people whose identity was summed up in such simple words as: "Writ and made up by a mother of seven hongry [sic] children."

The most memorable of the Dust Bowl songs, however, were written by a folk musician named Woody Guthrie, a man who would become known as "the Dust Bowl troubadour." As the folklife experts at the Library of Congress have stated, "Perhaps the lone salvation of human tragedy is that occasionally it finds its poet, the one person who lends enduring meaning to suffering and rescues dignity from disaster. The Dust Bowl crisis . . . found its poet in Woody Guthrie."

A native of Oklahoma, Guthrie was living in Texas when the full effects of the Dust Bowl began to be felt. "There on the Texas plains," he wrote, "right in the dead center of the dust bowl, with . . . the wheat blowed out and the hard-working people just stumbling about, bothered with mortgages, debts, bills, sickness, worries of every blowing kind, I [saw] there was plenty to make up songs about."

Make them up he did, songs with such titles as "The Great Dust Storm," "Dust Can't Kill Me," and "Dust Bowl Refugee," songs written in the Dust Bowl and on the road as Guthrie joined the migrants on the trek to California. Most important, they were songs that not only decried the Dust Bowlers' troubles but also described their courage. As John Steinbeck said, "There is nothing sweet about the songs [Woody Guthrie] sings. But there is something more important. . . . There is the will of a people to endure and fight against oppression. I think we call this the American Spirit."

Above: *Music was one of the few pleasant diversions the Dust Bowl migrants could enjoy during their difficult trek to California.*

Opposite: *Through the songs that he wrote—such as "This Land Is Your Land," one of the most famous folk songs ever created— the music of Woody Guthrie continues to inspire new generations of Americans.*

Those Who Stayed

"Dad always lived with hope. . . . 'Next year. Next year. I failed this time, but next year'll be better.' And I never did see him have the look of givin' up or quitting."
—TEXAS FARM BOY MELT WHITE

The images that photographers captured of the Dust Bowl victims on the road and in California were so powerful that, even years later, many of those who viewed them had the impression that almost all those in the stricken region had fled out of desperation. That was not the case. More than two-thirds of those who lived in the Dust Bowl chose to stick it out. Why did they do so? Some, like Nettie Featherston, lacked the means to leave. Others stayed out of loyalty to the land. Still others simply refused to give up. Most who remained and fought it out did so because of a faith in the future—the belief that things were bound to improve.

Staying truly meant fighting it out. For many farmers that meant spending hours plowing away the huge amounts of dust that lay in the fields. "Every dime I got is tied up right here," one farmer stated. "If I don't get it out, I've got to drive off and leave it. Where would I go and what would I do? I know what the land did once for me, maybe it will do it again."

Even if they were able to clear the fields, attempting to plant a crop meant working amid the ever-present dust, never knowing if a major dust storm would cover everything up again. But still they tried. "I guess I've made 1,000 miles right up and down this field in the dust when you couldn't see . . . and had to use headlights," the farmer on the opposite page explained. "This soil is the best there is anywhere, but it sure does blow when it's right. If you stay in the house and wait for the dust to stop you won't make a crop."

Above: *Removing the dust that was continually blowing and drifting was in itself a full-time job. Here, a farmer shovels away the dust that, if left unattended, would completely bury all his fence posts.*

Opposite: *For many farmers, the act of continuing to plow even during dust storms was their way of showing that, no matter what happened, they would not be defeated.*

A Symbol of Enduring Courage

"[My photograph] made people realize that here was a tragedy that was affecting people—it wasn't just affecting crops." —ARTHUR ROTHSTEIN

"**Arthur Rothstein,**" photography critic Cecil Beaton wrote, "made a masterpiece when he was sent out to document the plight of the farmers whose land had been devastated." The masterpiece to which Beaton was referring is the photograph on the opposite page—an image titled "Fleeing a Dust Storm," which, like Dorothea Lange's "Migrant Mother," became a symbol of the entire Dust Bowl experience. Unlike Lange, who concentrated in great measure on photographing those who had fled from the Dust Bowl, Arthur Rothstein—who was the first photographer that Roy Stryker hired for the FSA—took pictures of those who chose to remain on their land no matter how difficult the situation became.

In order to take the most revealing photographs possible, Rothstein moved to the Dust Bowl and took pictures every day. And it was while he was wandering through a farm in Cimarron County, Oklahoma, that he captured his most well-known image—that of a farmer and his two sons walking past a shed during yet another dust storm. "I had no idea at the time that it was going to become a famous photograph," Rothstein later stated. "It was a picture that had a very simple kind of composition."

Its composition may have been simple, but to almost all who saw it, the picture symbolized what those in the Dust Bowl were going through and the courage that even the youngest members of the family were continually called upon to display. Commenting on the photograph, the curators in the Library of Congress's photography division wrote, "While conveying the desolation of the land and the isolation of the people, it also underscores the stalwart attitude of the farmer and his sons as they move against a wind so full of dust the photographer could hardly breathe."

Like "Migrant Mother," "Fleeing a Dust Storm" helped bring about change. "[It] had a great deal of influence on people in the East . . . who had . . . no sense of identity with this poor farmer," Rothstein later said. "And it helped . . . provide legislation for soil conservation to remedy these conditions."

Above: *This photograph that Arthur Rothstein took in Bel Grade, Florida, thousands of miles from the Dust Bowl, became a different kind of icon—a symbol of the bounty that the American soil could bring forth if it was not abused.*

Opposite: *"Fleeing a Dust Storm" was one of a number of Dust Bowl photographs that helped photography gain further recognition as an art form. This photograph was eventually prominently displayed in New York's Metropolitan Museum of Art.*

Coping with Hardship

"'Dust to eat,' and dust to breathe and dust to drink. Dust in the beds and in the flour bin, on dishes and walls and windows, in hair and eyes and ears and teeth and throats."
—OKLAHOMA FARM WOMAN CAROLINE HENDERSON

Never in the nation's history had people endured so much in a heroic effort to remain on their land. Even as the dust storms continued to roll in and their crops continued to fail, thousands of families refused to give in. They used their ingenuity to survive. With no money available for their growing children's clothing, mothers took down their curtains or cut up flour sacks and used this material to make clothes for their youngsters. Once a family member's shoes wore out, they were resoled with rubber from used-up automobile tires.

With little or no crops available to eat or sell, feeding the family was an even greater challenge. For months at a time many families existed mainly on turnips and potatoes, the only food that managed to survive in the devastated soil. Some resourceful women resorted to picking and canning wild grasses and weeds such as dandelions and serving them much as they would serve vegetables.

Many families managed to keep their chickens alive and they could count on the eggs they produced, but feeding the cows vital to their survival was another matter. Fortunately some families discovered that the roots of the once-scorned yucca plant that grew wild in the region could be dug up and ground into a nourishing substance that could keep the cows alive.

It was all an extraordinary demonstration of a willingness to do whatever it took to hold on to the land. For many, however, it was not enough. Years later, Marguerite Dunmire, a teacher in the Dust Bowl area of Nebraska, would recall a particularly poignant moment. Noticing that a little girl in her class was looking pale and weak, she told the student to go home and have some food. "Oh, I can't do that," the child replied. "Today is my sister's turn to eat."

Above: *No matter how severe the dust storms were, constant attention had to be paid to the livestock, which were particularly vulnerable to the effects of the choking storms.*

Opposite: *With no money to buy new clothes, garments were continually mended to make them last as long as possible. Here, a young girl repairs a rip in one of her parents' articles of clothing.*

Vacation from Reality

"Toto, I have a feeling we're not in Kansas anymore." —THE WIZARD OF OZ

At first glance, one of the most surprising facts about the Great Depression and Dust Bowl era is that during this poverty-stricken time more people went to the movies than ever before. For the millions struggling to survive, finding a way to escape from the realities of their situation for even a little while became very important, especially since television had not been invented yet.

At a cost of about ten cents a ticket, movies offered one of the least expensive ways to take a vacation from one's troubles. And during the 1930s, as many as 75 million people a week went to the motion pictures. Moviemakers, well aware of what was bringing such extraordinary crowds to the theaters, quickly turned to making movies that helped people escape into a fantasy world totally different from their own. By watching films in which members of high society enjoyed all the pleasures of the good life, for at least a couple of hours moviegoers could pretend to be part of a life they would never know.

Not surprisingly, one of the most popular movies of the decade was *The Wizard of Oz*, a total flight from reality in which a young girl and her dog are magically transported from Kansas, the heart of the Dust Bowl, to a fantasy land. Also popular were *Snow White and the Seven Dwarfs*, the first of the Three Stooges movies, Shirley Temple's plucky adventures, and the horror film *Frankenstein*—all movies designed to help people forget their troubles for at least a little while.

Along with motion pictures, song sheets with the lyrics to popular tunes that sold for only a nickel also became popular, allowing people to gather together and spend the night singing. Board games were also just catching on, and at the height of the dust storms, an out-of-work heating-equipment salesman named Charles Darrow invented a game that allowed millions to play at becoming rich by acquiring valuable real estate. He called his game Monopoly, a Dust Bowl– and Great Depression–era phenomenon that has continued to be the most successful board game of all time.

Above: *One of the most popular of all the 1930s fictional characters created to take moviegoers' minds off their troubles was the heroic "King of the Jungle"—Tarzan.*

Opposite: *This sign advertises the current movie playing in Pinal County, Arizona, at the Dust Bowl Theatre. The movie house was so named because so many people living in the area were Dust Bowl refugees from Oklahoma and Texas.*

DUST BOWL THEATRE

"TARZAN'S SECRET TREASURE"

IT'S ALL NEW!

WITH

Johnny WEISSMULLER

MAUREEN O'SULLIVAN

SUN.-MON.

Everyone Pitches In

"A horse sale was held . . . in the afternoon. I sold one of [our horses]. There are six left now, I don't know how long I can keep them." —Nebraska farmer Don Hartwell

Nothing better illustrated the willpower, pride, and optimism that characterized those who chose to remain in the Dust Bowl than the farmers' determination to keep working the land despite the realization that the next dust storm could arrive at any moment. It was a courageous undertaking, but a dangerous one as well. "If Dad was in the field we were always afraid, you know," recalled young Lorene White. "We didn't know whether Dad could get in or not because the dust was so bad."

Actually, there was very little time for youngsters like Lorene White to spend being afraid. For, like their parents, they had responsibilities essential to the survival of the family. The children fed the chickens and collected their precious eggs. They milked the cows. Several times a day, it was their job to clear the dangerous dust from the nostrils of all the livestock. Then each dawn it was their responsibility to check that none of the animals had suffocated to death on the dust during the night.

Young people also had another important responsibility. The continuous drought had caused the wells of most of the Dust Bowl farms to run dry, and water had to be hauled in—sometimes from a great distance. The children's help in hauling the precious water was essential. "We had a team and we had water barrels," recalled Melt White. "We hauled [water for animals] and household water both. . . . Lots of mornin's we'd get up and strain our drinkin' water . . . to strain the [dust] out of it. But then, of course, a lotta [dust] went through and settled to the bottom of the bucket, but you had to have drinkin' water. . . . You didn't take a sip and throw it away, . . . it was a very precious thing to us because we had to haul it."

Above: *The young people's responsibility for feeding and caring for the chickens was extremely important. With their fields covered in dust, the only income many families received was through the sale of the eggs that their chickens laid.*

Opposite: *Oklahoma youngsters enjoy a rare moment of relaxation before returning to their important chores. Because their labors were so badly needed, none of the children in this photograph had ever been to school.*

A Remarkable Optimism

"We have faith in the future, we are here to stay." —KANSAN ADA BUELL NORRIS

As conditions continued to deteriorate, many families finally ran out of money and could not keep up their payments to the bank each month. "[I had put all my money] in what I thought was the best investment—the good old earth—but we lost on that, too," stated a Nebraska farmer, who had done everything he could to hold on since the dust storms began. "The mortgage company caught up with us," he told a Dust Bowl photographer. "[I] managed to lose twelve thousand dollars in three years."

Others also lost their land and were forced to stand by sadly as their farm machinery and livestock were auctioned off. Yet most farmers still refused to leave the region, convinced that better days lay ahead. Many moved into makeshift dwellings in the area. To make whatever money they could, the women took in washing or mended clothes. Wherever possible, the men took on part-time work on other farms.

"The plains people," historian Donald Worster wrote, "were a tough-minded, leather-skinned folk, not easily discouraged." It was an incredible understatement. Despite all they had endured, the majority of those who clung to the region maintained their remarkable optimism. As the *Dalhart Texan*'s editor John L. McCarty would write, "Conditions are going to be much brighter and better, and when they are we will hardly realize what has happened."

Above: *Auction posters like this one advertising the sale of farm machinery and livestock were a daily reminder of the obstacles many families faced in their bid to hold on to their farms.*

Opposite: *Somehow, the woman standing in the doorway managed to smile as her picture was taken, even though, as the sign on her Oklahoma City dwelling tells us, she had been forced to take in "washings" and "iornings [sic]."*

Dust Bowl Humorist

"The farmer has to be an optimist or he wouldn't still be a farmer." —WILL ROGERS

He was a cowboy, a rodeo and stage performer, a movie star, an author, and a radio personality. His name was Will Rogers, and during his lifetime he was the single most popular and beloved person in America. Most of all, he was a man with an extraordinary wit and sense of humor, who could make people laugh even during the most troubled times.

Many of his comments became legendary. Proud of his Cherokee heritage, for example, he stated, "My forefathers didn't come over on the *Mayflower*, but they met the boat." Particularly fond of poking fun at the United States Congress, he declared, "Every time they make a joke it's a law. And every time they make a law it's a joke."

Millions of people would take delight in Will Rogers's comments, but those who chose to remain in the Dust Bowl appreciated him most. "Everything is funny," he proclaimed, "as long as it is happening to somebody else." Throughout their ordeal, they found comfort and encouragement in his down-to-earth humor and the compassion he obviously had for them. Before the first dust storms had appeared, Rogers, with his typical wit, advised his fellow Oklahomans, "Buy land. They ain't making any more of the stuff." The Dust Bowlers particularly

appreciated how, when the hard times set in, he focused his humor on issues that pertained directly to them through such comments as, "Last year we said, 'Things can't go on like this,' and they didn't, they got worse."

It was more than humor—it was wisdom that enabled people to get through the worst of times. Wisdom that enabled Will Rogers to sum up the extraordinary experiences of those who remained in the Dust Bowl by stating, "The best way out of a difficulty is through it."

Above: *Will Rogers performs his most famous cowboy trick by throwing three ropes at once—one around the neck of a horse, another around the horse's rider, and a third around the horse's four legs.*

Opposite: *Will Rogers traveled around the world three times, made seventy-one movies, and wrote more than 4,000 newspaper columns.*

Humor in the Midst of Adversity

"In the middle of the dry years, it got so hot that hens were laying hard-boiled eggs."
—POPULAR DUST BOWL TALL TALE

One of the most extraordinary aspects of the entire Dust Bowl experience was the fact that those who stayed in the region not only learned to cope but actually managed to poke fun at their situation. The tall tales and jokes that emerged from the Dust Bowl years soon became an integral part of American folk humor. There was, for example, the story of the Oklahoman who fainted from the shock of having a drop of rain hit him; he was revived by having three buckets of sand thrown in his face. There was the joke about the farmers in Kansas now having to pay real-estate taxes in Texas because that's where their farms had blown. Other tall tales included accounts of fish wearing goggles to keep the dust out of their eyes and birds flying backward for the same reason.

Perhaps the most popular of all the tall tales was the one about the Dust Bowl motorist who suddenly encountered a ten-gallon hat perched upon a dust drift. When the motorist lifted the hat he found a face staring at him. "Can I help you in some way?" the motorist asked. "Give you a ride into town maybe?" "Thanks," replied the buried man, "but I'll make it on my own. I'm on a horse."

It was humor born out of the necessity to keep their will and spirits up in the face of extraordinary adversity. And the greatest champion of all in that regard was John L. McCarty, editor of the newspaper the *Dalhart Texan*. McCarty formed the Last Man Club, printing up enrollment cards that read: "Barring Acts of God or unforeseen personal tragedy or family illness, I pledge myself to be the Last Man to leave this country, to always be loyal to it, and to do my best to cooperate with other members of the Last Man Club."

Above: *It was in the southern plains towns that farmers gathered together to swap the latest Dust Bowl humorous stories and to ask the question that remained on everyone's lips— "When do you think it will rain?"*

Opposite: *Laughing at adversity, often to soothe the pain of troubled times, has long been an American trait. Never was this more in evidence than during the Dust Bowl days.*

Rain at Last

"Three little words achingly familiar on a Western farmer's tongue rule life today in the dust bowl of the continent. If it rains." —ROBERT GEIGER, *WASHINGTON EVENING STAR*

In 1939, the Dust Bowl farmers' prayers were, at last, answered. Just as abruptly as the rain had ceased almost a decade before, the skies opened up. First came showers, and then a more constant downpour. And it kept on raining. Slowly but surely the southern plains came back to life. "When the rain came, it meant life itself. It meant a future. It meant that there would be something better ahead of you," young Floyd Coen would later explain. "And we, as young people and sometimes parents, you'd go out in that rain and just feel that rain hit your face. It was a very emotional time when you'd get rain because it meant so much to you. You didn't have false hope anymore, you knew then that you was going to have some crops."

Young as he was, Coen was right. Within weeks of the arrival of the rains, the dry fields, as shown in the photograph on this page, were rejuvenated.

The farmers and their families were not the only ones overjoyed that the rains had finally come. The photographers, who had lived among them and had shared their anguish as they battled against such overwhelming odds, were enormously relieved as well. Now they could begin taking very different kinds of pictures, photographs that revealed how the rains that brought a blossoming of the crops also did the same to the spirits of those who had been struggling to grow them. The photograph of the father and son on the opposite page was typical of this new type of image, pictures that symbolized rekindled hope in the land and confidence that things would be much brighter—especially for the young people of the southern plains.

Above: *With the return of steady rains, the southern plains came to life again, producing scenes like this one, of fields of wheat so bountiful that people working in them were practically lost to view.*

Opposite: *By meeting every challenge that remaining in the Dust Bowl had presented, this farmer and millions like him had given the nation yet another lesson in courage and determination.*

The Tree Army

In his March 4, 1933, inaugural address, President Franklin D. Roosevelt stated, "Our greatest . . . task is to put people to work. This is no unsolvable problem if we face it wisely and courageously. It can be accomplished in part by direct recruiting by the Government itself, treating the task as we would treat the emergency of a war, but at the same time, through this employment, accomplishing greatly needed projects to stimulate and reorganize the use of our national resources."

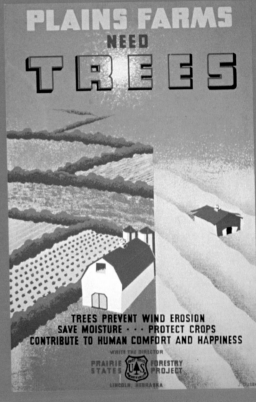

This dual goal—putting people to work and saving our natural resources, particularly the soil—became the basis for one of the most successful of all the government's relief and reform projects. It was called the Civilian Conservation Corps (CCC) and it was carried out, beginning in 1933, by millions of young people between the ages of seventeen and twenty-three.

The CCC initially enrolled 250,000 young men, but by the time it was disbanded in 1942, some three million had taken part in its important work—not only in every U.S. state but in several of the nation's territories as well. During its nine years of service, the CCC would be called upon to make many contributions to the betterment of the nation. As far as President Roosevelt was concerned, however, its most important goal was to help restore the soil in the Dust Bowl region through the planting of trees that would serve as barriers against wind erosion. Before their work was done, the members of what became fondly known as "Roosevelt's Tree Army" planted an extraordinary three billion trees—not only establishing the hoped-for wind barriers but providing the people of the Dust Bowl region with a vital demonstration of how measures could be taken to prevent future dust bowls from occurring.

Above: *This poster, created by the WPA's innovative poster division, heralded all the benefits that farmers would receive from the planting of trees throughout the plains.*

Opposite: *The U.S. government stated that the Civilian Conservation Corps was "a young man's opportunity for work play study & health." Here, young CCC workers prepare once-untillable soil for the planting of trees.*

Saving the Land

> *"Out of the long list of nature's gifts to man, none is perhaps so utterly essential to human life as soil."* —HUGH HAMMOND BENNETT

Fortunately there were others in the government besides President Roosevelt determined to prevent another calamity like the Dust Bowl. Among them was Hugh Hammond Bennett, a man destined to become known as "the father of soil conservation."

Long before the Dust Bowl tragedy, Bennett had been one of the few to express his alarm at the way the southern plains farmers were using up the land. As early as 1928 he had written, "An era of land wreckage destined to weigh heavily upon the welfare of the next generation is at hand." Over the next five years Bennett traveled the country tirelessly, giving speeches designed to awaken Americans to the need to save their soil. "What would be the feeling of this Nation," he exclaimed, "should a foreign nation suddenly enter the United States and destroy 90,000 acres of land, as erosion has been allowed to do in a single county?"

In 1935, thanks in great measure to his speeches and the scores of articles he wrote pleading for government action to save the land, Congress established the Soil Conservation Service (SCS) and named Bennett its chief.

Under his direction, the SCS established programs designed to introduce farmers to agricultural practices that would conserve, rather than destroy, the soil. By the time his career was over, Bennett had dedicated more than fifty years of his life to saving the country's most precious resource and making it a national priority. As famous conservationist Louis Bromfield wrote, "Hugh Bennett deserves the greatest honor from the American people as one of the greatest benefactors since the beginning of their history."

Above: *FSA photographer Marion Post Wolcott captured this scene of farmers engaged in contour plowing, a soil-saving procedure taught to them by government agricultural experts.*

Opposite: *These two photographs were taken two years apart in the exact same spot in Beadle County, South Dakota. The first, shot in 1935, shows the barns surrounded by six feet of sand. The second, taken in 1937, shows the dramatic effect of proper soil and moisture-saving farming methods.*

Faces of the Dust Bowl

"Many of these people were sick, hungry, and miserable. The odds were against them. Yet their goodness and strength survived." —ROY STRYKER

Even as we plan to conserve our precious natural resources, we must always remember the people of the Dust Bowl—the men, women, and young people who were the victims of the first ecological disaster in our nation's history. In the face of extraordinary hardships, these people either put down new roots more than half a continent away or succeeded in clinging tenaciously to their native soil.

They lived through a remarkable decade, unique in the nation's history. It was also an extraordinary decade as far as photography was concerned. By informing the nation of the plight of so many of their fellow citizens, the FSA photographers played a vital role in bringing about needed change. They recorded the anguish, but they also provided the visual proof of the indomitable spirit of the American people, even in the face of extreme adversity.

As far as Roy Stryker was concerned, this spirit could be seen best in the faces of the people that his photographers recorded. "The faces to me were the most significant part of the [photographs]," he wrote. "When a man is down and they have taken from him his job and his land and his home—everything he spent his life working for—he's going to have the expression of tragedy permanently on his face. But I have always believed that the American people have the ability to endure. And that is in those faces, too."

In the motion picture version of *The Grapes of Wrath*, Ma Joad, the character that John Steinbeck created to symbolize the courage of the Dust Bowl women, perhaps provided the best summary of all. "We're the people that live," she states. "They can't wipe us out. They can't lick us. We'll go on forever . . . 'cause we're the people."

Sources For Opening Quotations

Many of these sources are listed with full bibliographic data elsewhere in the back matter. For those, I provide only the author/speaker name, year of the quote, and title of the original source material, to avoid repetition. For those sources that do not appear elsewhere, I provide full bibliographic data here.

Page 4: Dorothea Lange, 1936. *Dorothea Lange: Photographs of a Lifetime*

Page 6: John Greenleaf Whittier, 1854. *Complete Poetical Works of John Greenleaf Whittier.* Whitefish, Montana: Kessinger Publishing, 2003.

Page 8: Caroline Henderson, 1931. *Letters from the Dust Bowl*

Page 10: Abraham Krames, 1938. Interview with the author, 1955.

Page 12: Ann Marie Low, 1936. *Dust Bowl Diary*

Page 14: Charles Dana Wilber, 1881. Wilber, Charles Dana. *The Great Valleys and Prairies of Nebraska and the Northwest.* Omaha, Nebraska: Daily Republican Print, 1881.

Page 16: Kathleen (Allen) Lewis, 1932. Ochiltree County Sesquicentennial Committee. *Wheatheart of the Plains: History Marches On.* Perryton, Texas: Ochiltree County Sesquicentennial Committee, 1985.

Page 18: Anonymous Kansas farm woman, 1935. *Dust Bowl: The Southern Plains in the 1930s*

Page 20: Avis D. Carlson, 1935. Stutz, Bruce. *Chasing Spring: An American Journey Through a Changing Season.* New York: Scribner, 2006.

Page 22: Unknown Associated Press reporter, 1935. *Liberal News* (Liberal, Kansas). 1935. Church crowd in panic as Liberal Beclouded. April 14.

Page 24: Ann Marie Low, 1934. *Dust Bowl Diary*

Page 26: Unknown author, 1934. *The Worst Hard Time*

Page 28: Aaron Siskind, circa 1945. Lyons, Nathan. *Photographers on Photography.* Upper Saddle River, New Jersey: Prentice Hall, 1966.

Page 30: Walt Whitman, 1865. Whitman, Walt. *Leaves of Grass.* Garden City, New York: Doubleday, Page and Company, 1919.

Page 32: E. Y. (Yip) Harburg, 1931. Harburg, Yip. *The Yip Harburg Songbook.* New York: Warner Brothers Publishing, 1994.

Page 34: Franklin Delano Roosevelt, 1933. *Inaugural Addresses of the Presidents of the United States.* Washington, D.C.: U.S. G.P.O.: for sale by the Supt. of Docs., U.S. G.P.O., 1989; Bartleby.com, 2001. www.bartleby.com/124/. [January 7, 2009].

Page 36: Sherman Berger, 1934. Interview with the author, 1955.

Page 38: Roy Stryker, circa 1945. Parker, Paul E. *A Portrait of Missouri, 1935–1943: Photographs from the Farm Security Administration.* Columbia, Missouri: University of Missouri Press, 2002.

Page 40: Ben Shahn, 1936. Pastan, Amy, ed. *Fields of Vision: The Photographs of Ben Shahn.* Washington, D.C.: D. Giles Ltd. and The Library of Congress, 2008.

Page 42: Russell Lee, 1936–1939. Griffith, Vivé. "Compassionate Lens," The University of Texas at Austin Feature Story. http://www.utexas.edu/features/2007/lee/. [January 7, 2009].

Page 44: Anonymous Kansas preacher, 1936. *Children of the Great Depression*

Page 46: Lawrence Svobida, 1936. *Farming the Dust Bowl: A First-Hand Account from Kansas*

Page 48: Dorothea Lange, 1935. *Dorothea Lange: Photographs of a Lifetime*

Page 50: Dorothea Lange, 1935. *Dorothea Lange: Photographs of a Lifetime*

Page 52: John Steinbeck, 1939. *The Grapes of Wrath*

Page 54: Imogene Glover, 1998. "Surviving the Dust Bowl," written and produced by Chana Gazit, coproduced and edited by David Steward. A film for *The American Experience*, produced by WGBH Boston, MA, 1998. http://www.pbs.org/wgbh/amex/dustbowl/filmmore/transcript/transcript1.html.

Page 56: Anonymous Dust Bowl migrant, 1936. Caption accompanying a Dorothea Lange photograph, Library of Congress.

Page 58: Edward Steichen, 1939. *Documenting America, 1935–1943*

Page 60: Anonymous Texas migrant farmer, 1938. Caption accompanying a Dorothea Lange photograph, Library of Congress.

Page 62: *Life* magazine credo, 1936. "The World According to Luce." American Masters, Thirteen, WNET, New York. http://www.thirteen.org/pressroom/pdf/am/luce/AMLuceQuotes.pdf.

Page 64: Franklin Delano Roosevelt, 1937. *Inaugural Addresses of the Presidents of the United States.* Washington, D.C.: U.S. G.P.O.: for sale by the Supt. of Docs., U.S. G.P.O., 1989; Bartleby.com, 2001. www.bartleby.com/124/. [January 7, 2009].

Page 66: Woody Guthrie, 1935. Lomax, Alan. *Hard Hitting Songs for Hard-Hit People.* New York: Oak Publications, 1967.

Page 68: Melt White, 1998. "Surviving the Dust Bowl"

Page 70: Arthur Rothstein, 1964. Oral history interview with Arthur Rothstein, 1964 May 25, Archives of American Art, Smithsonian Institution.

Page 72: Caroline Henderson, 1935. *Letters from the Dust Bowl*

Page 74: Dorothy Gale (movie character), 1939. *The Wizard of Oz*, directed by Victor Fleming, produced by Mervyn LeRoy, 1939.

Page 76: Don Hartwell, 1936. *The Worst Hard Time*

Page 78: Ada Buell Norris, 1941. Hope, Clifford R., Sr. "Kansas in the 1930s." *Kansas Historical Quarterly* 36 (Spring 1970, No. 1).

Page 80: Will Rogers, circa 1935. Rogers, Will, and Ayres, Alex. *The Wit and Wisdom of Will Rogers: An A-to-Z Compendium of Quotes from America's Best-Loved Humorist.* Edited by Alex Ayres. New York: Meridian, 1993.

Page 82: Anonymous, circa 1935. Botkin, B.A. *A Treasury of American Folklore: Stories, Ballads, and Traditions of the People.* New York: Crown Publishers, 1944.

Page 84: Reporter Robert Geiger, 1935. Logsdon, Guy. "Dust Bowl Lore." Oklahoma Historical Society's Encyclopedia of Oklahoma History & Culture. http://digital.library.okstate.edu/encyclopedia/entries/D/DU012.html. [January 9, 2009].

Page 86: Franklin Delano Roosevelt, 1933. Roosevelt, Franklin Delano, and E. Taylor Parks. *Memorable Quotations of Franklin D. Roosevelt.* New York: Crowell, 1965.

Page 88: Hugh Hammond Bennett, 1939. Bennett, Hugh Hammond. *Soil Conservation.* New York: McGraw–Hill Book Company, Inc., 1939.

Page 90: Roy Stryker, 1973. *Documenting America, 1935–1943*

Key Sources

The following sources have been particularly important in presenting key concepts in this book:

Timothy Egan's *The Worst Hard Time: The Untold Story of Those Who Survived the Great American Dust Bowl* describes how more than two-thirds of those in the Dust Bowl chose to remain rather than flee to California and other West Coast states and how they struggled to survive.

Carl Fleischhauer and Beverly W. Brannan's *Documenting America, 1935–1943,* and Pete Daniels, Merry Foresta, Maren Stange, and Sally Stein's *Official Images: New Deal Photography* provide insight into the photographers who documented the Dust Bowl experience, the nature of their images, and the ways in which their pictures helped bring about reform.

Donald Worster's *Dust Bowl: The Southern Plains in the 1930s* remains the classic study of the causes of the Dust Bowl, the nature of the dust storms, the migration of hundreds of thousands of people, and the need for conservation of the American soil.

The Library of Congress Archives:

The Farm Security Administration (FSA) photographs of the Dust Bowl experience, and many of their accompanying captions, have been an invaluable source in creating this book. All of the FSA images are housed in the Library of Congress. You can view and study the Dust Bowl pictures in the following manner:

Go to the following URL: http://www.loc.gov/rr/print/catalog.html

Next, click on the blue box labeled *Search the Catalog.*

Here are some key terms you can enter into the search bar at the top of the page to get you started: *Lange, Migrants; Lange, California; Dust Bowl; Rothstein, Arthur;* and *Lee, Russell.*

Here is a bibliography of the most significant sources I used in my research:

Coles, Robert. *Dorothea Lange: Photographs of a Lifetime.* New York: Aperture, 2005.

Daniels, Pete, Merry Foresta, Maren Stange, and Sally Stein. *Official Images: New Deal Photography.* Washington: Smithsonian Books, 1987.

Egan, Timothy. *The Worst Hard Time: The Untold Story of Those Who Survived the Great American Dust Bowl.* Boston: Houghton Mifflin, 2005.

Fleischhauer, Carl, and Beverly W. Brannan. *Documenting America, 1935–1943.* Berkeley, California: University of California Press, 1988.

Gregory, James. *American Exodus: The Dust Bowl Migration and Okie Culture in California.* New York: Oxford University Press, 1989.

Henderson, Caroline. *Letters from the Dust Bowl.* Norman, Oklahoma: University of Oklahoma Press, 2001.

Lomax, Alan. *Hard Hitting Songs for Hard-Hit People.* New York: Oak Publications, 1967.

Stryker, Roy, and Nancy Wood. *In this Proud Land: America, 1935–1943, as Seen in the FSA Photographs.* New York: Graphic Society, 1973.

Svobida, Lawrence. *Farming the Dust Bowl: A First-Hand Account from Kansas.* Lawrence, Kansas: University Press of Kansas, 1986.

Watkins, T. H. *The Hungry Years: A Narrative History of the Great Depression in America.* New York: Henry Holt, 2000.

Worster, Donald. *Dust Bowl: The Southern Plains in the 1930s.* New York: Oxford University Press, 2004.

Photo Credits

Further Reading and Surfing

Books for Young Readers

Cooper, Michael. *Dust to Eat: Drought and Depression in the 1930s.* New York: Clarion Books, 2004.

DeAngelis, Therese, and Gina DeAngelis. *The Dust Bowl.* New York: Chelsea House, 2001.

Egan, Timothy. *The Worst Hard Time: The Untold Story of Those Who Survived the Great American Dust Bowl.* Boston: Houghton Mifflin, 2005.

Freedman, Russell. *Children of the Great Depression.* New York: Clarion Books, 2005.

Henderson, Caroline. *Letters from the Dust Bowl.* Norman, Oklahoma: University of Oklahoma Press, 2001.

Hesse, Karen. *Out of the Dust.* New York: Scholastic, 1997.

Low, Ann Marie. *Dust Bowl Diary.* Lincoln: University of Nebraska Press, 1984.

Partridge, Elizabeth. *Restless Spirit: The Life and Work of Dorothea Lange.* New York: Viking Juvenile, 2001.

Sandler, Martin. *Pioneers.* New York: HarperCollins, 1994.

Stanley, Jerry. *Children of the Dust Bowl: The True Story of the School at Weedpatch Camp.* New York: Crown Books for Young Readers, 1993.

Steinbeck, John. *The Grapes of Wrath.* New York: The Viking Press, 1939.

Svobida, Lawrence. *Farming the Dust Bowl: A First-Hand Account from Kansas.* Lawrence, Kansas: University Press of Kansas, 1986.

Worster, Donald. *Dust Bowl: The Southern Plains in the 1930s.* New York: Oxford University Press, 2004.

Web Sites

http://www.pbs.org/wgbh/amex/dustbowl/

http://lcweb2.loc.gov/learn/features/timeline/depwwii/dustbowl/dustbowl.html

http://www.nychumanities.com/DustBowl.html

DVDs

American Experience: *Surviving the Dust Bowl.* Produced and written by Chana Gazit. Boston: WGBH Educational Foundation, 1998.

The Grapes of Wrath. Directed by John Ford. Los Angeles: 20th Century Fox Studios, 1940.

The Plow That Broke the Plains. Written and directed by Pare Lorentz. Washington DC: National Archives, 1936.

Index

For Christopher, Sarah, Winslow, Robert, and Lila Re,
who are discovering that anything is possible

Acknowledgments

Once again, this book would not have been possible without the way in which Emily Easton has shaped it, guided my efforts, and edited it well beyond the call of duty. I am indebted also to Mary Kate Castellani for her many valuable contributions to this book. I am most grateful for the beautiful design that Donna Mark and Alyssa Morris brought to this volume, as well as the assistance I received from Mark Lewis of the Library of Congress, Katherine Worten, and my agent, John Thornton. And I owe many thanks to historian *par excellence* Russell Potter and to Melissa Kavonic for so thoroughly checking the accuracy of every page. As always, Carol Sandler has been not only an invaluable contributor but an inspiration.

First published in the United States of America in 2009 by
Walker Publishing Company, Inc.
Visit Walker & Company's Web site at www.walkeryoungreaders.com

For information about permission to reproduce selections from this book, write to
Permissions, Walker & Company, 175 Fifth Avenue, New York, New York 10010

Quotes on page 52 from *The Grapes of Wrath* by John Steinbeck published by Penguin Great Books of the 20th Century

Library of Congress Cataloging-in-Publication Data
Sandler, Martin W.
The Dust Bowl through the lens : how photography revealed and helped remedy a national disaster / Martin W. Sandler.
p.   cm.
ISBN-13: 978-0-8027-9547-2 • ISBN-10: 0-8027-9547-1 (hardcover)
ISBN-13: 978-0-8027-9548-9 • ISBN-10: 0-8027-9548-X (reinforced)
1. Dust Bowl Era, 1931–1939—Juvenile literature. 2. Great Plains—History—20th century—Juvenile literature. 3. Farmers—
Great Plains—History—20th century—Juvenile literature. 4. Dust Bowl Era, 1931–1939—Pictorial works—Juvenile literature. 5. Great Plains—
History—20th century—Pictorial works—Juvenile literature. 6. Farmers—Great Plains—History—20th century—Pictorial works—
Juvenile literature. 7. Documentary photography—United States—History—20th century—Juvenile literature. I. Title.
F595.S24 2008   973.917022'2—dc22   2008055979

Book design by Alyssa Morris
Typeset in Monotype Fournier and Letter Head Fonts Bell Boy
Printed in China by WKT Printing Co. Ltd.
2 4 6 8 10 9 7 5 3 1 (hardcover)
2 4 6 8 10 9 7 5 3 1 (reinforced)

All papers used by Walker & Company are natural, recyclable products made from wood grown in well-managed forests.
The manufacturing processes conform to the environmental regulations of the country of origin.

NEBRASKA

COLORADO

KANSAS

OKLAHOMA

NEW MEXICO

TEXAS

KEY

DUST BOWL REGION

NOV   2009